# WISDOM SERIES ON HUMILITY, PRIDE & STRENGTH

CHARLES AWODU

# Endorsements

Without doubt this is a teaching book that extols the virtues of humility, pride and strength and concurrently excoriates the vices inherent in their misuse or abuse in a penetrating, readable comparative analysis.

No wonder Mr. Awodu, a cerebral youth coach, mentor and leadership aficionado, is deliberative in targeting this literary contribution towards the youth, his primary area of calling, to help them "catch and run" with their vision early in life. And by so doing, he has provided them with a handy pathway to avoid the 'common' pitfalls that have crashed many a destiny.

Indeed, this is a book of immeasurable value to serve as a guide post to successful fulfillment of destiny.

Parents and youths are encouraged to grab copies to digest. I believe it is worth the investment.

Segun Olanipekun, PhD.
Lead Consultant/Editor,
CMNL Consulting Ltd

I have the honor of having Charles Awodu as my student in two different courses under the title "Leadership". I went through the details of the Book *Wisdom Series on Humility, Pride & Strength*.

I am amazingly surprised by Charles' understanding and insightfulness into the deep realities of life we face all along. I have enormous respect for his dedication and his determination to make quality education accessible to less privileged children. I am also aware of Charles' great knowledge and skills, as well as of the hard work he devotes to humanitarian causes.

It has been a privilege to know Charles, and I endorse this book wholeheartedly. This endorsement note cannot stress enough Charles' dedication and hard work.

Dr. Ifa Khan
Lecturer: Northeastern University, Boston MA

Charles Awodu enlightened our minds in this book with a picture of life as a coin with two sides: the positive and negative. He made it clear that we should not allow other peoples' opinions to box us into a stereotype of negativity. According to him, humility has the positive side that exalts and the negative side that promotes silence in the face of tyranny; pride has the positive side of generating passion for excellence and the negative side that leads to failure, destruction, and so on. With this analogy, Charles Awodu brings these facts onto the front burner to encourage the younger generation not to allow their potential to be limited or killed by the negative opinions of others. Congratulations Charles for a job well done.

**Seyi Macaulay PMP**
**President, Dreamyouth International**

This is one of those rare materials that would espouse humility as strength and describe pride from the perspective of godliness. Not too many writers consider humility as a strength. I have read motivational books, but I have seen few so lucid, so flowy, and yet so loaded with wisdom for existential living. What stands out about this book is the simplicity of writing and by extension the magnetic way of communicating to various categories of people; and of course, the fluidity of language. I recommend it to those seeking the good and godly life.

**Prof. Sheriff F. Folarin**
**Covenant University, Ota, Ogun State, Nigeria**

Juxtaposing between the conventional understanding of humility, pride and strength with a deep insight of the three concepts, Charles Awodu is challenging the modern generation to be unapologetic in claiming their identity in all its beauty and ashes.

Charles is a beloved child of God, a man of integrity, a creative writer and speaker, and a leader par excellence. I am grateful for his passion and determination to inspire the minds of future world leaders for a life of excellence, significance, and greater productivity.

In this book, Charles invites you to be proactive with your inner strength, step out of your comfort zone and do what others have claimed cannot be done. *"There is a product or service in you, waiting to be discovered and deployed to meet someone's need. Money comes from providing solutions."* Charles uses the power of creativity, innovation, inspiration, and beautiful poetry to challenge humanity to maximize their potential. May you be blessed by this masterpiece.

**The Reverend Dr. Moses O. Sowale**
**President of The Voice Inc.**

# Acknowledgement

We are products of what we learned from others. I am grateful to God and all sources through whom I have drawn inspiration to write this book: my Professors, Mentors, Teachers, Pastors, Parents, friends and family.

My special appreciation goes to my wonderful wife and kids for their understanding and cooperation while working on the manuscript of this book. I can't but appreciate our coaching crew at World Leadership & Inspirational Foundation Inc. for their encouragement in writing this book.

I am indeed grateful to all who saw this possibility in

me and encouraged me to keep taking steps in converting my potentials into products for the benefit of mankind.

# Dedication

To Gary C. Link, a friend and dreamer, who escaped a ghastly motor accident during Covid-19.

To young dreamers and leaders of tomorrow.

And to all dreamers whose lives were cut short by Covid-19

# Foreword

*P*ride is often regarded as a negative disposition but it can be seen as a trait for excellence and expression of aroma of achievements. While the former can lead to distrust and condemnation, the latter can build trust and confidence.

Strength is about ability, inner energy and inherent resources. It is raw materials for qualitative and first class service delivery in someone. It is a quality needed for performance and achievement of results. Humility is a meekness spirit. It is the opposite of pride. A humble spirit is lowly in disposition, notwithstanding his or her high profile strength and achievements in life.

The author has demonstrated his creative writing style in this book to help readers discover the various qualities of life needed for positive human relationships.

I have known the author for couple of years now and I can see his zeal in helping all categories of humans to possess the ingredients needed for effective living, and I am bold to expressly support his positive ideas, ideals and possibility thinking.

This book will stimulate your earnest interest and desire to be better in your human relationship management vis-à-vis the components needed for achievement of excellence in life.

I wish to recommend the book to both growth and fixed mindset individuals, hoping that more resources will be gathered for added values and positive living.

John B. Ajewole
Chief Editor,
The Word of Life Publications Co.

# Introduction

The United Nations' estimate of the world's population in 2019 revealed that there are about 1.2 billion youths aged 15-24 years, or 16 percent of the global population. The number of youths in the world is projected to grow by 7 percent to 1.3 billion by 2030.

The youth population in the poorest countries is projected to increase 62 percent by 2050. This calls for the need to write this book that will help open the minds of the youths to recognize their strengths and pursue them in humility, to provide solutions to human problems and bring pride to their various societies and nations.

The wrong interpretation of pride, humility and strength to the younger ones by selfish leaders, teachers and mentors limits and sullies the gift that God has placed in most youths, even more than the effects of economic stagnation in the world. Hence, the need for a copy of this book for every youth and young dreamer.

The push for self-discovery in our youths to bridge the institutional gaps in our nations is of great importance if we desire a society free from social vices as the population of the world grows.

Youths are leaders of tomorrow, and we must teach and write to ignite their consciousness to prioritize converting their youthful strengths into products and services that benefit humanity, very early in life.

I strongly recommend this book for students, young graduates and adults who want to live their full potential in life. A copy for any youth is a huge investment in their uncommon transformation. Read, reflect and act on the content of this book. It is your turn to get informed to achieve uncommon transformation. Let's go!

# Contents

# Humility

"There is no need to show off when you know who you are."

-Maxime Lagace

# Short Illustrative Lesson To Learn About Humility

A story was told of a rich man and his pastor. This pastor does not have as many material things as the rich man, but he lacks nothing that a pastor should have.

No doubt, he preaches the truth and lives what he preaches. Most often, his ministration sounds offensive to this rich man. As a result, the rich man hates his pastor and always encourages others to work against his good intentions to move the church forward.

The rich man was able to influence others in the church to keep working against the pastor.

This rich man was appointed to head a public post where he served 4 years. At the end of his tenure, another person took his position and a lot of irregularities were discovered to have taken place during the period that this rich man served.

His records of performance were investigated and he was found guilty of corrupt practices. He could have avoided this if he had allowed the teachings of the Pastor to find expression in his life.

The rich man ended his career in shame, instead of using the opportunity to repent from his evil ways through the word of God that he had been receiving from his pastor.

The lesson from this short story is that you

should not allow your wealth to make you work against the word of God. Let it be a great privilege to influence others to live a humble life.

It is indeed a truth as the book of wisdom says, "pride goes before destruction and haughtiness before a fall, better it is to be of a humble spirit with the lowly, than to divide the spoil with the proud."[1]

# What Is Humility?

**H**umility is the submission to God's will in other to live a life of relevance. It is believing that God has the final say as you do your best daily. It is being lowly in spirit and being teachable without thinking less of yourself. Humility is your ability to submit yourself in *truth* for God's sake to serve people. It makes you real and allows you to never live in pretense. True humility is evidence of exceptional courage.

Take, For instance, Nelson Mandela's fight for freedom in South Africa. He knew what his people deserved as designed by God, and chose to go for it, not minding what people might say or feel about it.

He was not afraid to consciously sacrifice for freedom, which is God's expectation for mankind.

*"Humility is the noble choice to forgo your status, deploy your resources or use your influence for the good of others before yourself. A humble person is marked by a willingness to hold power in service of others."* [2]

Humility is indeed a great power when it is not exercised in ignorance. It takes being honest with yourself to be able to live a humble life. Humility is an intentional sacrifice and learning process. It is not humility if it is not adding value to you. Humble people are teachable people, they entertain constructive criticism and corrections and never submit to deceptions. They are not weak but very strong and smart.

*"A true student is like a sponge. Absorbing what goes on around him, filtering it, latching on to what he can hold. A student is self-critical, self-motivated, always trying to improve his understanding so that he can move on to the next topic, the next challenge."* [3]

Humble people build in themselves the mentality that every person they meet knows something that they don't know. They have a learning heart through which they generate an exceptional attitude for a life of excellence.

Humility is recognizing who you are and who others are. It is your ability to respectfully question what is wrong for possible redirection.

Sometimes, it causes you not to follow the popular way or support failing standards or trends. Humility is indeed a common sense, expressed in truth and in a timely manner for the purpose of serving humanity. It is an attitude you display under someone you trust to avoid abuse.

It is not humility when you override truth with kindness. *For instance, your inability to respectfully question what is wrong in others in order to keep winning favor from them, or to keep saying 'Yes' to everything your boss says even when they are wrong, is not humility in service but weakness.* Humility is nothing but living in truth.

Always learn to walk in humility but with good

conscience. It is this kind of humility that attracts divine inspiration for uncommon direction in life, most especially when you are surrounded by enemies, false accusers or selfish bosses. Humility as a key can open so many doors that a haughty spirit can't. The humble place is the place of uncommon possibilities, learnings and redirections.

## What Humility Is Not

Humility is not supporting injustice or anything that does not comply with godly principles, excellence or truth simply to satisfy a superior authority.

It is not degrading yourself each time someone passes a compliment. *Imagine, someone may say you are smart, handsome or beautiful and you reply, "No sir/ma'am, I am not", just to display how humble you are as a person. It is better to politely say, thank you sir/ma'am.* While too many compliments can ignite person's ego, a simple acknowledgement of a pleasant compliment is not a display of ego, but a stylish rejection of pleasant compliment is a sign of inferiority complex.

Humility is not pretense but truth. It is not when you reduce yourself to nothing before men. It is a show of courage to drive your self-worth and do what is right. What we called "humility" in some cultures are signs of weakness in another. *For instance, in some African cultures, looking into your elders' or seniors' eyes in a discussion is a sign of rudeness or lack of humility, but in America or some other developed nations it can be seen otherwise. If you pay attention as you work with others in a highly diverse organization, you might observe this as people relate with one another.*

Your inability to verbalize your convictions in a respectful manner is not humility but self-abuse. Sometimes, people will be dying deep within, but they won't express their need to be helped, heard or rescued. Many have wasted their lives through this behavior. Don't be one of them. Be bold enough to ask questions for clarity at any time. *The acceptance of pre-planned expectations of men as against your conviction in God is not humility, it simply reflects the fear of men over God. This is very common in religious places.*

The exercise of humility is not a sign of weakness, but an attitude of grace, strength and excellence. It makes people look like angels or act as a children of God.

Humility is not forgetting your worth. It is not thinking less of yourself but thinking of yourself less. You don't consider yourself to be worthless as proof of humility.

Humility is not exercising patience in ignorance. Humility is not self-projection behind the scenes. Humility does not carry an iota of pride in disguise.

It is not choosing to go with the crowd or being a life follower when you have the capacity to create, lead or drive possible change. Humility is a core trait of an exceptional leader.

Humility is not feeling inferior to anyone. This understanding is necessary as it has been instructed in the Word of God.

*"But I have understanding as well as you; I am not inferior to you: yea, who knoweth not such things as these."* 4

Humility in truth sets free. It makes you trust God and have self-confidence. No exercise of humility keeps anyone in captivity if it is done in truth.

> **"And ye shall know the truth and the truth shall make you free."** [5]

Humility can be abused. This may be the case if you see any of the following signs in others:

Uncontrollable fear, self-doubts, oppression, humiliation, unhappiness, the inability to ask questions, etc.

## Steps To Exercise Humility

Everyone needs humility to sustain success, hence the need to take the below steps when among others.

- ☆ Learn to count your blessings and be thankful;

- ☆ Recognize when you need help and seek it out;

- ☆ Develop an "I-don't-know-it-all" mentality;

- ☆ Learn to re-examine your actions. If your action is not yielding profit, value or progress, check your quality of humility or obedience;

- ☆ Match your words and actions with results in

your environment;

☆ Learn to admit when you are wrong and say sorry. This can be a bit more difficult for a boss than a leader;

☆ Seek feedback from people regularly;

☆ Be open to other peoples' viewpoints.

## The Prize Of Humility

Humility adds value to you. It brings great honor to you and to others.

*"God resists the proud and gives grace to the humble. Therefore humble yourselves under the mighty hand of God, that He may exalt you."* [6]

When you humble yourself God will exalt you.

God always lifts up the humble. Your humility can cause people around you to want to help you. Humility can lead to business breakthroughs or promotions.

People cherish those who are making an impact in life - those who combine humility with excellence.

They can rise to the defense of such a person at all times. We have seen good politicians that people keep supporting for so many years because of their consistent positive impact, and we have seen those who never finish a term or win a bid for re-election.

Humility attracts people's trust. Humility can't be exercised outside of love, trust or truth. It is a good attitude that makes leadership interesting.

Humility is self-help because it boosts your self-control over the challenges of life.

It gives opportunity to trust and learn from God for possible direction.

*"Trust in the Lord with all your heart; do not depend on your own understanding. Seek his will in all you do, and he will show you which path to take."* [7]

# *Pride*

*"Pride must die in you, or nothing of heaven can live in you."*

-Andrew Murray

## An Illustrative Story To Learn About Pride

*A story was told of a pastor with a great congregation. What greatly distinguishes his church from others is its talented choir. The choir members are very young and filled with passion for singing, and the choir is led by two individuals, one male and one female. John was the head and Janet the deputy. Janet and John trained many others who could replace them, as is the custom of any responsible leader.*

*After serving the Church for 12 and 15 years*

respectively, a time came when John and Janet started to think of having their own bands to follow their God-given purpose. They prayed and built relevant skills to power their purpose in order to extend the glory of God to the world using their talents. They were convinced of their revealed vision.

They called their Pastor and told him their plans. The pastor said, I will pray about it. They waited for another three years for the Pastor to call them, but nothing came up.

Janet decided to start working out her strategies in boldness, but John, out of fear of the pastor's annoyance, decided to wait for the pastor. He did everything to please his pastor so he might earn a positive response. Each time he asked his pastor, the response he got was that God had not spoken.

John turned 75 years old and never thought of taking a further step because of what his pastor might say. He lost his vision, and regretted it at old age.

Janet, on the other hand, did not wait that long for her pastor. After 5 years of expecting his response, she started working on her vision because she found peace of mind about it.

While working on her vision, sometimes she would be invited to other churches and would need to be away from her church. She missed some activities in her church due to her self-development and engagement outside the church. During this time, her actions were considered as being proud and she was tagged Miss Pride. At the slightest opportunity her pastor would berate her good efforts as a negative influence.

Janet, because of her conviction, would not let all the negative opinions limit or ruin her zeal and passion. She endured until she left to build the future she desired. God raised helpers for her as soon as she took that bold step of faith to launch out.

Her pastor – who knew that Janet had not in any way offended him – made peace with her. At this time, Janet had become a great instrument of evangelism and a life transforming agent in the hand of God.

She became a pride to the gospel movement because her melodious songs revived souls. But John couldn't make any difference outside the four walls of his church due to fear and not wanting to be tagged Mr. Pride.

What ignorance! He regretted this when all his

strength was gone and a new person had to replace him.

From this story, we could see that deploying your talent for the glory of God is not a negative or bad pride.

# What Is Pride?

The first impression that readily comes to mind once the word "pride" is mentioned is "downfall", but not all pride leads to downfall.

*"There are two kinds of pride, both good and bad. 'Good pride' represents our dignity and self-respect. 'Bad pride' is the deadly sin of superiority that reeks of conceit and arrogance."* [1]

Pride as a double-edged emotion could mean a bloated ego, boasting, self-dependent, haughty spirit and behaving like you are better than every other person.

No one will do anything great in life without being driven by the desire to make a difference in life. This is a systemic nature of good or positive pride in a man. That is, striving to do what others can't or aren't willing to do.

Pride could also mean an urgent force that propels you toward building a good legacy. It pushes you for excellence and creativity. It could mean the urge to solve any stubborn problem that has defied a long-time solution. It is a catalyst for growth and development if positively exercised.

You just want to get something done to set the captive free. For instance, someone with a humble background who strives to break poverty's chain from his or her lineage. Anyone will feel good for achieving such an exceptional result. This kind of feeling is what drives every great achiever toward success, and that is the spirit of good pride. Every reasonable person strives daily to be his or her own best. This kind of drive is nothing but the desire to feel admired for doing a great thing, which is good pride.

No wonder Elijah Ihejiere, the 2021 overall best

graduating student of New Height Charter School in Brockton MA, said as interviewed, *" I knew honor and admiration awaits me, if I do my best"*. Positive pride is indeed the secret of success.

> *"Desire for pride is the motivation that underpins ambition. It makes us care about how others see us and – just as important – how we see ourselves. It makes us want to feel good about ourselves and make sure others look up to us, admire us, and see us as competent and powerful. It prods us to figure out who we want to be and then to do whatever is needed to become that person."* [2]

Pride can be positive or negative and can either build or ruin. It can be the feeling in you that ignites your consciousness to go and do extra work for your team to meet deadlines for collective success, or the feeling that without you, your team or another individual can't succeed.

Imagine these two statements: *You are too proud and I am proud of you.* The first one is condemnation while the other is commendation.

The history of pride as a negative disposition is traceable to Satan. He was called Lucifer but pride brought him low to become a Satan.

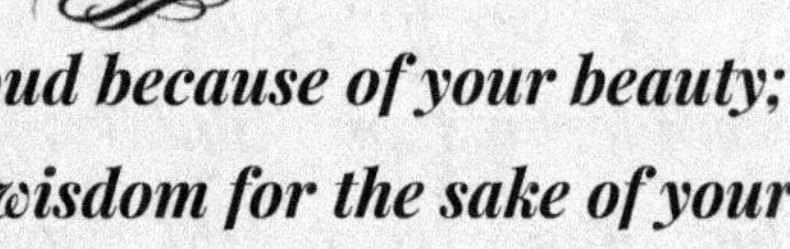

*"Your heart was proud because of your beauty; you corrupted your wisdom for the sake of your splendor. I cast you to the ground; I exposed you before kings, to feast their eyes on you."* [3]

Pride wrongly exercised as an emotion, has become one of the deadliest sins in the history of humanity. It is a haughty attitude and disposition of the heart.

It takes the garment of grace for man to overcome the spirit of pride. Whether positive or negative, if pride is not well managed it can lead to one's downfall and failure. We must not allow our pride to be our master but to serve us to live an excellent and impactful life.

*"High performers face a unique set of character traps because they are, by definition, outperforming so many around them. When you are succeeding beyond others, it's easy to get a*

> *big head. You can begin to think you're special, separate from, better than, or more important than other people... This is a way of thinking that you must avoid at all cost."*[4]

## Pride As An Instrument For Failure And Downfall

The man of pride can fail and fall if the emotion is not well managed. It amounts to pride when a man says "I am this or that" rather than saying "I am this or that by the grace of God. Fall is imminent and inevitable."

The fall of Lucifer was rooted in selfish ambition and negative pride. These, to date, are the common downfalls of men. Sometimes a man may say, I am going to do this and that tomorrow, without having regard for God who supplies grace for this accomplishment. You must be humble in the pursuit of your ambition.

> *"How you have fallen from heaven, O Star of the morning, son of the dawn! You who have been cut down to the earth, you have weakened the nations! But you said in your heart, "I will ascend to heaven; I will raise my throne above*

> *the stars of God; and I will sit on the mount of assembly in the recesses of the north; I will ascend above the height of the clouds, I will make myself like the Most High."* [5]

If you begin to see yourself as the only tree in the forest of achievement, with no regard for any other person or opinion, you might be on the verge of falling.

A man of pride can fail when left to himself to exhaust his self-will, ego, self-satisfaction and self-importance to the brim. Such a person may crash-land, leading to shame and self-delusion.

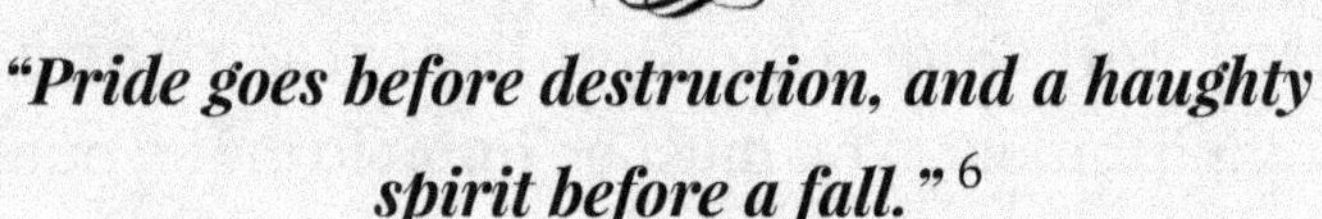

> *"Pride goes before destruction, and a haughty spirit before a fall."* [6]

A man who was aspiring for a political office with a haughty spirit once declared that his opponents were too small to match his worth. The day the names of his opponents were made public, he declared that with this quality of people, victory at the polls would be his. He paid musicians and sent invitations to friends ahead of time to get set for the celebration. He relied on false surveys of his popularity and undermined the potential support of the electorate for his opponent during the polls. This man eventually lost to one of his opponents. ***This is a big lesson never to look down on or write others off because of your privilege, ambition or position.*** Do a good job instead, recognize your competition, and be humble.

## Pride As An Instrument For Motivation And Commitment

Pride inspires you to be a good example to others, a person of honor worthy to be emulated and referenced for excellent works. You need your pride to become a great person in life. Don't trash it to please anyone, but be humble. Pride is the outcome of uncommon sacrifice.

The positive side of pride can be the expression of 'I can' and not 'I am.' A man with excellent spirit may express gallantry over being triumphant, with full assurance that given another chance, he might still achieve the same feats.

It is an attitude traceable to one's ability to accomplish a task or meet set goals. It has a lot to do with self-confidence, excellence and competence.

The pride here becomes an instrument of commitment and motivation to do more.

Pride can be a driving **tool of motivation** for the wise, but this also depends on the individual's **orientation** to it.

*Take for instance: The motivation to take your shower as you set out for the office or any other social event is not just for maintaining good health alone, but to also maintain a neat and clean appearance in the midst of your peers. This feeling of recognition or satisfaction is a form of pride that every reasonable person naturally and emotionally displays every day.*

Pride makes you strive to be part of the winning team. It makes you go after anything of significance that meets people's needs. Every reasonable person wants to feel included, honored or respected in any system, and this inspires them to give their all in pursuit of a goal that will benefit others, in order to attain honor through the positive impact. It encourages them to be creative, or to develop their talents to live their full potential. Well-managed pride draws uncommon blessings, growth and development through creativity. This drive to feel honored helps a dreamer know when to increase his or her momentum or change mentality towards making positive impacts capable of influencing others to do well.

## What Pride Is Not

It is not when you know your strength and reject any human opinion that sounds contrary to it, or putting your best into what you do in an uncommon way. It is not when you are honest or authentic about something you believe in.

It means maximizing the gifts and potential of God in you. It means having the consciousness to pursue excellence. It means telling others about the things of God. It means being bold and smart, to walk with the wise or those who have gone before you in your area of interest. It means being able to understand and pursue your uniqueness to separate yourself from the crowd.

It means having faith-filled ambition to make a difference in life. It means resisting ignorance, superstitions and oppression.

It is not pride to do same thing in a different way and be a change maker.

It is not impossible for you to be wrongly accused in life for maximizing your strength. It happens, but you only need to allow the positive nature of this emotion called pride push you through to succeed in what you do. This kind of accusation is very common at the beginning of discovering your purpose or talent in life. The desire to live a fulfilled life can't but cause you to depart from some conventional ways of doing things that people might term arrogance, disobedience, rudeness or an ulterior motive, but the possibility of becoming a change maker, path finder or a good influence should be strong enough to make you overcome this season that tests your strength.

## Forms Of Bad Or Negative Pride

Boasting, ego, pomposity, haughtiness, self-willfulness, arrogance, incorrigibility and boasting over one's gifts and talents are all forms of negative pride.

Pride, amongst others, includes:

☆ Being self-sufficient/over-confident. Remember, a tree doesn't make a forest. A singular person can't make a success. You need others of like mind;

☆ Talking about yourself only;

☆ Inability to publicly appreciate good works of others;

☆ Uncontrollable self-condemnation for an inability to meet your own standards;

☆ Inability to say that you don't know something;

☆ Considering everyone too low to learn from or belittling others;

☆ Hating corrections, no respect for anyone;

☆ Easily embarrassed or wanting to impress or oppress others.

## Forms Of Good Or Positive Pride

Pride can be: An emotion that pushes you to be more and not less, or the deep inner thoughts or drives that remind you that there is yet untapped potential in you that needs to be uncovered. The force of this emotion propels you toward excellence, significance and greater productivity in making change happen. It won't just make you rest in your comfort zone.

People in the developed world place great priority on positive pride while in some developing nations, due to cultural and religious influences, less is being done to ignite the consciousness of people about positive pride. Even though the people show it, the awareness is not as great as in the developed nations. This emotion has a lot to do with creativity.

Striving to solve problems that have defied long term solutions, like early in the year 2020 when the world urgently needed a solution to COVID-19.

Being able to re-write an unpleasant story for good.

The ability to successfully rescue someone from undeserved frustration or a life-threatening circumstance.

Seeking to volunteer for a good cause in your community.

Striving to defend your nation against internal and

external threats.

Being able to work to become who you said you will be in life.

Becoming a responsible citizen that people can refer to as a role model in the community and nation.

The good outcome of your effort is a positive pride. *For instance, becoming the first graduate in a specific field of study with honors after seeing that none has ever achieved such a feat in the history of your family. I myself am the first graduate, both first and second degree in Accounting & Leadership respectively, in my family. In my family more focus is on sciences than other disciplines. I did as well in my sciences as in my art classes but chose to do what has not been done before in an excellent way, and I do not regret it.*

## Causes Of Negative & Positive Pride

Feeling that you have an especially unique breed of personality, or not recognizing that someone else can match one's strength and ability through gaining special privileges and having some talents, gifts, financial and educational edge over others is one of the common causes of negative pride.

On the other hand, the need to live an impactful life, leaving a good legacy behind wherever you find yourself and becoming a responsible ambassador, change maker, and inventor are some of the common causes of positive pride.

## Dealing With Pride

☆ Identify your strengths and seek help for your weaknesses;

☆ Build experts with the fear of God around you;

☆ Understand that every teacher needs a better teacher. Get a mentor or coach;

☆ Understand when to delegate;

☆ Don't look down on people or possible competition;

☆ Observe weird ideas for possible gains;

☆ Learn to say sorry or adjust;

☆ Look inward to discover your positive pride and ask God to show you ways to harness the principle associated with your positive pride.

*Avoiding pride is not the issue but sacrificing to make the right kind of pride possible is all that matters.*

## Reflections: How May We Describe The Following Cases?

- ☆ When someone thinks differently and has the boldness to take relevant steps on his or her conviction;

- ☆ When people label you ignorantly and seek to recruit forces to stop you;

- ☆ When seeking to be transformed from old ways as life changes to do what is right or fulfill your purpose;

- ☆ When realizing the work of God in you and declaring it to propel internal and outward moves;

- ☆ When striving to be the pride or role model of your family, community, organization and so on.

Chapter Three

# *Strength*

"You were given this life because you are strong enough to live it."

-Felix H.

# An Illustrative Story To Get Started With

*"Think and don't listen to people who tell you it can't be done. Life's too short to think small."*

*– Tim Ferriss*

This reminds me of a story about a man named Jack, who left his country in search of greener pasture after winning the American visa lottery. He had a good job while in his country, before he resigned and left for the unknown in the United States of America as an immigrant.

His expectation was that he would get a better job as quickly as possible, due to the picture the media had painted about the opportunities in the U.S., but unfortunately, it was a different story when he got there. After searching for jobs in his area of expertise for months without success, a friend advised him to settle for any job that came his way, pending the time a better opportunity would come. He felt reluctant at first, but later made up his mind to join his friend working as a janitor.

He felt very frustrated as he considered the job he had while in his home country to be more dignified, and he told his friend this. This circumstance forced him to think about discovering himself. It was indeed a moment of pain that forced him to discover the raw gold in him waiting to be heated by fire before it comes out shining to command greater price.

One day he had a moment for deep reflection about his passion of becoming a doctor. It started when he was in elementary school in his country. He called his friend who helped him got his present job and told him about his plan of going into a medical school, but he couldn't get any positive encouragement from his friend about it.

He was advised that it would take a long time to finish and he doesn't need to overstress himself, but he refused to listen to the voice of negativity and rather he chose to settle for the consequences of his conviction. The following day, he took a step of faith to call a nearby university to inquire about his options. After his enquiry, he applied and followed through with the process to study medicine. He was accepted after a few months.

He endured the process and successfully finished his course, and later got a better job. As he was practicing, he was helping the less privileged in his community and participating in various volunteer activities and town hall meetings, and he became well known for his positive contributions in the community. Eventually, he contested a senatorial seat and won.

This story clearly shows, as Brain Tracy once said, that, "fear and self-doubt have always been the greatest enemies of human potential". If Jack had entertained fear or doubted himself he wouldn't have become a man of great influence. Never accept giving up as your next option no matter your present condition; success is possible if you think you can succeed. Develop yourself to adapt to your new environment for relevance. There's always a *potential yet untapped in you. Don't settle for less. Something more is in you; find it and it will make you.*

# What Is Strength?

It means having inherent abilities and inner treasures such as talents, giftedness, potential, intelligence, skillfulness, brilliance and ingenuity.

All these can be traced to natural, mental and physical abilities which are connected to the use of heart, head and hands.

Examples of strengths are having the ability to write, sing, dance, create, build, design, motivate, lead and inspire others.

Everyone is created with unique strength, and in your strength lies the power to create. You either learn to create or create to learn. If strength is not developed to be deployed it will remain dormant for life. Strength can be invested, misdirected or wasted.

Not everyone places much value on their strength. It must be noted that prayer alone won't develop your strength, it must be intentionally worked out.

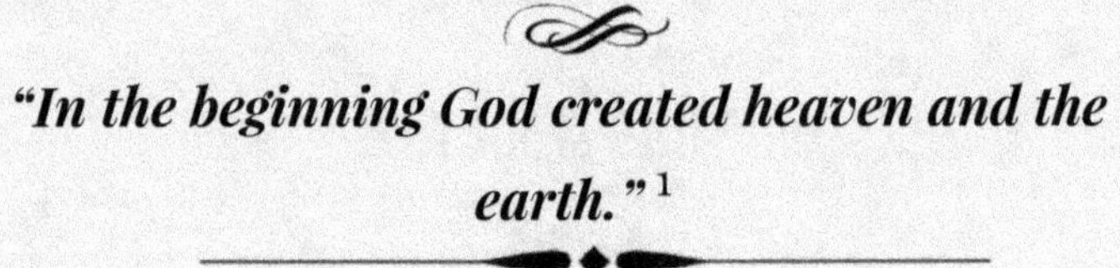

> *"In the beginning God created heaven and the earth."* [1]

The word "created" here means worked.

Did God see in verse 31 that everything He created was good? Yes, He did. So, engaging in religious activities without working to experience the future you see is a risk.

Strive daily for the best and don't settle for less. If you are careless with your talent or strength, others will take advantage of it, at your expense.

## How And Where To Identify Your Strength

☆ Lifelong learning;

☆ Positive environments;

☆ When things are tough and rough;

☆ Passionate pursuits;

☆ Asking people to tell you. It takes humility to do this;

☆ Reflect and refrain from any effort that is not leading to progress or profit;

☆ Be feedback conscious.

## What Strength Is Not

It is not being crafty, wayward, reckless, and excessive, or being pompous.

It is not selfishly taking advantage of others.

It is not an opportunity to deny others of what they deserve.

It is not causing divisions or hatred where love should be promoted.

It is not hindering the possibilities of other people, but igniting them.

*A story was told of a company that was expecting expansion. In the following month, it was their strategic plan to promote staff* members who had been there for five years and passed the required professional qualifications.

This company has in its production unit four staff, namely: Jack, Young, Hack and Stone. It happened that Young consecutively observed errors in the material compliance reports that Hack prepared in the last two quarters and reported it to their manager. Hack, being a pompous senior colleague, was not happy about it. Hack had spent 7 years with the company and Young 3 years.

Hack, having read the company's strategic plans, discovered that he was the only person that qualified for the planned promotion exercise. He discussed with Stone that once he got promoted to a higher role where he had the power for departmental appraisal reports he *would do all he could to write Young off and if possible ensure her demotion or dismissal. What a wicked mentality!*

*This is misuse of positional strength and must be discouraged in any system that is bound to succeed. Higher roles by ethic are designed to bring the best out of people, and not frustration for doing well. It must be used never to promote discrimination in any disguise.*

## Identifying Your Strength

*"The greatest threat to being all you could be is satisfaction with who you are."*[2]

A songwriter says his strength is built on nothing less than Jesus' blood and righteousness. God has made everything possible but wants you to take responsibility in truth, having confidence in yourself as you believe God to find your way to these treasures.

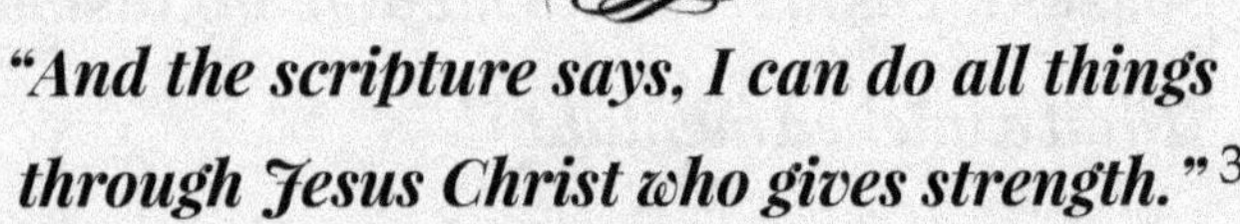



The available grace at your disposal is an indication that you possess the strength that is greater than your needs. This treasure is in you and until you find it, life remains a frustration.

You must recognize that you possess generational and life-changing treasure in you that must not be wasted. You can change something for the better with the potential in you.

Sometimes, it takes disappointment or pressure enforced by unpleasant situations to propel us to discover our area of strength or talents. This should be a conscious desire of everyone. Don't wait until your youthful strength is exhausted before you start thinking of developing your potential.

## Creativity And Strength

Identifying your strength is *good*, converting it to products or services to meet people's needs is *better*, and getting returns from it is the *best*. This has a lot to do with your ability to create. You must learn to *create* and create to *learn* if you want to succeed in life. There is a product or service in you, waiting to be discovered and deployed to meet someone's need. Money comes from providing solutions.

> *"...All it takes to be creative, then, is an inner assurance that what I think or do is new and valuable."* [4]

You need to be sensitive to your environment and fence your strength from being corrupted by the negative opinion of others, thereby placing limitation on your creative capabilities or talent. Fear of possible failure, the unknown or doubts can be injected into you. You can be influenced to disown your strength and possibilities.

As you pray for your country to get better, develop your strength to create something that can provide jobs and sources of income to people and your country as well. This is what makes your prayers work. Be creative as you pray. A locked up potential won't add value to anybody. Think until you think through.

God always speaks as you pray to do something; pay attention and learn to act on your good ideas. Do away with the mentality of waiting religiously for Him to come down to take responsibility for what He has empowered you to do.

A lot of answered prayers are locked up in the ideas that He sends your way every day, prompting you to act upon them for your uncommon transformation.

*"And he has filled him with the Spirit of God, with skill, with intelligence, with knowledge, and with all craftsmanship to devise artistic designs, to work in gold and silver and bronze."* [5]

Praying is listening, as thinking is doing. Don't engage in any of these exercise in ignorance. They are designed by God to generate results. There must be something that measures the efficacy of these two daily routines, **praying and thinking**. Unreleased potential is a great disservice to humanity. Arise, work and pray to release yours.

Fight your fear, because it remains the most terrible force against dream fulfilment. Fear of failure, men and the unknown is a trap that can mess up the essence of living; feed your potentials instead.

*Let me illustrate this with this short story of a woman, who after studying hard for her Bachelor's degree in Nursing was so scared to go for her board exam because she did not want to fail. She never practiced until she summoned courage to write, and passed the exam eight years after graduation. Eight years in a trap! Fear can be terrible. Fear got her stuck, limited and worried for a good eight years.*

Not all fear is bad; some fear can be of benefit. The fear of God is a positive fear, but the kind of fear expressed in the story above is a negative fear. Such fear that causes someone to cheat on an exam, fear of being infected during Covid-19, the fear of jumping down from an airplane without parachute, the fear of begging when one refuses to work. The fear of falling into sin and many more. How you manage your fear matters a lot.

## Developing Your Strength

Every good result takes time and success is a process, not an overnight miracle. God gave you a unique purpose with strength to make it happen, but you need an idea to convert it to reality. Sincerely speaking, every great change or transformation begins with an idea.

> *"God has tied our destinies to the quality of ideas that flow through our minds. Man can never rise above the quality of his ideas. This whole world was first an idea in God's mind before it became a reality. Hence an idea is the beginning of the process of creations."* [6]

You are a gifted individual. As you grow in grace and in the knowledge of Christ your strength is being developed beyond your expectations.

This won't be without challenges. Of course, challenges are catalysts for possibilities, depending on the quality of your thinking and the mercy of God. Every good thing attracts opposition and envy that you need courage and faith in God to overcome. Never settle to be a burden, work to live your full potential by working against every limitation on your way.

Think God first, as you build capacity to be more. Faith in God is not negotiable if you want to see the reality of your potentials. A strength becomes a burden for everyone when it is not being used in a godly way.

If you allow the light in your strength to shine it can re-write your story in a better way. This light is the quality of the products that your strength produces.

Also, as you search for greater knowledge from the Bible, trying new experiences or opportunities, getting more skills, keeping an open-mind, attending seminars and reading of other books, practicing self-discipline, or asking for feedback, you are developing your capacity to do more.

*It is never a curse that those who refuse to develop their strengths will serve those who develop theirs. Rich or poor you are useful to someone in life. Strive to live a meaningful life.*

## Strength And Your Environment

Your environment can trigger your capacity to do better with the available resources at your disposal.

The fish draws more strength in water than on dry land. A bird draws more strength in the air when it is flying than on the ground.

Your environment can add impetus to your strength.

Also, your environment can mess up your strength, if you are being surrounded by negative people or those who underrate your capacity to make a difference due to color, age differences, sex, social status, religion and more. This happens a lot. Never forget that there are environments that can blur your vision, or hinder your success or opportunities.

*"In every society there are traditions, norms, social expectations, customs, and value systems that impact, shape, mold, suppress, control and in some cases, oppress the natural gifts, talents, capabilities and potential of its members."* [7]

The perspective of the people that surround you can determine a lot for your possibilities. In any environment you find yourself, choose to be a builder of destiny and nothing less. Resemble your creator who specializes in good works.

So, observe and act smart to build intimate relationship with God for constant guidance or redirection.

In the course of writing this book, I interacted with a few entrepreneurs to ask about their experiences at the commencement of their businesses. I observed that every one of them faced strong resistance, disappointment and frustration during this period, but one striking comment that one of them gave was that, ***going into a legitimate business was seen by people around me as going into the world, but I never allowed that truncate my vision because they don't understand it better than it was revealed to me.*** He further stated that creativity was not a popular concept in his environment then, but religious activities.

This is one of the reasons why most young believers in such an environment hardly live out their full potential. Some believe they have to be in church every day to show how serious they are with God, without creating time for productive thinking. He said, today he is 65 years old, and while his mates wait for pension, he is signing checks and donating to support good works. Sometimes, you need to follow your conviction with all sincerity, and prepare for its consequences in faith when you are young. *Seek daily to create something with your youthful strength, and never forget that you can live your maximum life without forsaking God.*

## Managing Strength, Opposition And Critics

Tough times don't last; it is tough people that do last. Persecution, opposition and criticism can be the instruments of baptism that can fuel your strength and capacity to do more than you have ever thought to do, if you possess positive mentality. In life, most often, good things attract opposition.

Also, you can do all things through Christ who supplies you the needed strength as you depend on Him and set more realistic goals.

*"They that know their God shall be made strong and they shall do great exploit."* [8]

## Posible Scenerios That Come With Maximizing Your Strengths

People will say you have ulterior motives; you will be seen as a possible failure.

You will have friends like enemies and enemies like friends. At least one person will stand firm with you.

You will have someone that truthfully corrects you, if your vision is genuine you will easily recognize this person.

Also, you might be hated for following your passion.

People might expect you to listen to them more than God. You need self-discipline to overcome this moment.

Some will try to weigh your worth, gain from it and seek to belittle it.

You will be called a disobedient person because pursuing your strength won't make you stand with the crowd or follow conventional ways.

Sometimes those who celebrate your strengths or potential might not be those in your immediate environment. Due to familiarity, it won't make any sense to them until it comes to fruition.

People might take steps to frustrate you, but these very steps could open doors for you. I have experienced this.

A well-maximized strength will naturally draw in resources that will fund it.

Peace comes with dream fulfilment. This makes one feel like a true child of God.

Remember: no guts, no glory. You need courage to drive purpose.

## Self Reflections

- ☆ What challenge are you most proud of, that has changed your life for the better?

- ☆ What motivates you to do good daily?

- ☆ Have you misinterpreted other people's strength as bad pride?

- ☆ What understanding have you gained about Humility, Pride and Strength that you would like to share with others?

- ☆ Has anything changed in your perspective after reading this book?

- ☆ What values define your identity?

- ☆ Do you often override truth with kindness

because of what people might say?

☆ What advice will you give to a young dreamer about pride, humility and strength?

☆ Who significantly influenced your thoughts on success when you first discovered your purpose? Can you still remember him/her?

☆ Do you believe that you have a product in you waiting to be released?

☆ How have you been investing your free time? Do you waste it with people who are adding no value to you?

☆ How did you discover your strength?

☆ Has anyone abused your humility?

☆ In what ways have your pride, humility and strength contributed to the growth of your society?

☆ How do you exercise humility? In fear, or faith?

☆ Do you exercise humility by overriding truth with kindness?

# Notes:

## Chapter One

1 Bible, Proverb 16:18-19 (King James Version)

2 John, Dickson (2011). Humilitas, Zondervan Michigan USA, Pg 24

3 Ryan, Holiday (2016). Ego is the Enemy, Penguin NY, Pg 40-41

4 Bible, Job 12:3 (King James Version)

5 Bible, John 8:32 (King James Version)

6 Bible, 1 Peter 5:5b-6 (New King James Version)

7 Bible, Proverb 3:5-6 (New Living Translation)

## Chapter Two

1 Brendon, Burchard (2017). High Performance Habits, Hay House Publishers, India, Pg 296.

2 Jessica, Tracy (2016). Pride: The Secret of Success, Mariner Book, Houghton Mifflin Harcourt Publishing Company.

3 Bible, Ezekiel 28:17 (English Standard Version)

4 Brendon, Burchard (2017). High Performance Habits, Hay House Publishers, India, Pg 299.

5 Bible, Isaiah 14:12-14 (New American Standard Bible)

6 Bible, Proverb 16:18 (King James Version)

## Chapter Three

1 Bible, Genesis 1:1 (New International Version)

2 Myles Munroe (2008). Maximizing Your Potential, Destiny Image Publishers Shippensburg PA, Pg 13

3 Bible, Philippians 4:13 (New King James Version)

4 Mihaly Csiikszentmihaly (1997). Creativity, Harper Collins Publishers, Pg 25

5 Bible, Exodus 31:3 (English Standard Version)

6 Sam Adeyemi (2000). Ideas Rule The World, Pneuma Publishing Lagos Nigeria, Pg 83

7 Myles Munroe (2008). Maximizing Your Potential, Destiny Image Publishers Shippensburg PA, Pg 17

8 Bible, Daniel 11:32b (New King James Version)

# World Leadership & Inspirational Foundation Inc.

ounded and incorporated in 2018 as a non-profit and tax-exempt 501(c)(3) organization, World Leadership and Inspirational Foundation Inc. (WLIF) was a reaction to the pathetic state of misery, degradation and gross decadence pervading the gamut of human existence globally, the cause of which is largely traceable to poor and inept leadership. WLIF is therefore an antidote to eliminate or reduce this downward spiral in global leadership through the deployment of a set of tested, proven and creative training templates.

With an avowed commitment to combat some of the negative consequences of poor leadership, namely violence, banditry, suicide, insecurity and poverty, through vigorous and pragmatic training programs, WLIF is thus poised to attain its founding objective by raising vanguards of fresh, productive, reliable, entrepreneurial, result-driven and humane leaders in communities across the world, to inject the required doses of the antitode into the systemic structure of human societies for better outcomes.

Part of the proceeds of all books written by the founder, Charles Awodu, goes into the funding of this dream. Individuals or organizations that believe in this global transformation vision and would like to cheerfully support this dream can visit our website at **www.wolifoundation.org/donate. Thanks.**

Our training, enlightening, mentoring and coaching programs are being achieved through:

☆ **Lightning the Mind Seminars (Young Adults)**

☆ **Young Leadership Summit (Kids & Teens)**

☆ **Wisdom Notes Daily Broadcast**

☆ **Inspiring Moments**

☆ **Project Hope (Needy, Schools & Orphanages)**

☆ **Publications**

☆ **Weekly Inspirational Newsletter**
(www.wolifoundation.org/subscribe)

**For more information visit:**

www.wolifoundation.org or write

charles@wolifoundtion.org

**Instagram: nurturingtheminds**

# About The Book

This is a wisdom nugget book exposing the good and bad characteristics of Humility, Pride and Strength aimed at helping the readers to discover the qualities needed for positive relationships and an exceptional lifestyle.

Wisdom Series On Humility,
Pride And Strength

www.ingramcontent.com/pod-product-compliance
Lightning Source LLC
Chambersburg PA
CBHW050758160726
48004CB00002B/606